Informational Passages
for Text Marking & Close Reading

GRADE 1

By Marcia Miller & Martin Lee

NEW YORK • TORONTO • LONDON • AUCKLAND • SYDNEY
MEXICO CITY • NEW DELHI • HONG KONG • BUENOS AIRES

Teaching *Resources*

Cover design: Brian LaRossa
Interior design: Kathy Massaro

Photos ©: 14: Nanette Grebe/Shutterstock, Inc.; 16: Anthony Brown/Alamy Images; 18: Marie Appert/123RF;
20 left: smuay/ Shutterstock, Inc.; 20 right: worac/Thinkstock; 22: Florian Kopp/ImageBroker/Glow Images;
24 left: Alex Sobolevskiy/Shutterstock, Inc.; 24 right: Jorg Hackemann/Shutterstock, Inc.; 26: MBI/Alamy images; 28: natica/123RF;
30: Peshkova/Shutterstock, Inc.; 32: Yobro10/Thinkstock; 34 top: Vereshchagin Dmitry/123RF; 34 bottom: Philppe Renaud/123RF;
36: PavelRodimov/Thinkstock; 38 top: John Serrao/Science Source; 38 bottom: mmark86/Thinkstock;
40 top: Ardea/Jim Zipp/Animals Animals; 40 bottom: Richard Winston/Shutterstock, Inc.; 42: Nati Harnik/AP Images;
44: jarenwicklund/123RF; 46: phillyskater/iStock/Thinkstock; 48: Devon Ravine/NWF Daily News; 50: Courtesy Lulu Delacre;
52 left: Prapan Ngawkeaw/123RF; 52 right: koosen/iStockphoto.

ISBN: 978-0-545-79377-3
Copyright © 2015 by Scholastic Inc.
All rights reserved.
Printed in the U.S.A.
Published by Scholastic Inc.

2   3   4   5   6   7   8   9   10   40   22   21   20   19   18   17   16

Contents

> Informational Text Passages

Main Idea & Details

Sequence of Events

Fact & Opinion

Compare & Contrast

Cause & Effect

Problem & Solution

Introduction

The vast majority of what adults read—in books, magazines, or online—is nonfiction. We read news stories, memoirs, science pieces, sports articles, business e-mails and memos, editorials, arts reviews, health documents, assembly or installation instructions, advertisements, and catalogs. Informational reading, with its diverse structures, formats, and content-specific vocabulary, can be demanding.

Many students enjoy reading nonfiction, but navigating the wide variety of rich informational texts poses challenges for evolving readers. Students may lack sufficient background knowledge of a topic or be unfamiliar with specific vocabulary related to it. In addition, they may find some structures or features of nonfiction puzzling. This is why exposing students more frequently to informational texts and introducing them to active reading-comprehension strategies are now key components of successful reading instruction. Useful strategies, clearly taught, can empower readers to approach informational texts purposefully, closely, and independently. Such active tools provide students with a foundation for success not only in school, but for the rest of their lives.

> **Connections to the Standards**
>
> The chart on page 9 details how the lessons in this book will help your students meet the more rigorous demands of today's reading standards for informational text.

Text Marking: A Powerful Active-Reading Strategy

To improve their comprehension of informational texts, students must actively engage with the text. Careful and consistent text marking by hand is one valuable way to accomplish that. To begin with, by numbering paragraphs, students can readily identify the location of pertinent information when discussing a piece. By circling main ideas, underlining supporting details (such as definitions, descriptions, evidence, explanations, and data), and boxing key vocabulary, students interact directly with the material, making it more digestible in the process. But the true goal of teaching text marking is to help students internalize an effective close-reading strategy, not to have them show how many marks they can make on a page.

Purposeful text marking intensifies a reader's focus. It helps readers identify information as they read and recognize and isolate key details or connect relevant ideas presented in the text. For instance, boxing words like *first, next, then,* and *finally* can clarify the sequence of ideas or events in a passage. By circling expressions like *I think* and *I believe*, students learn to discern opinions from facts. When students are asked to compare and contrast information in a passage, boxing signal words, such as *both, but,* or *however,* can make identifying similarities and differences more apparent. Words like *since, because,* and *result* signal cause-and-effect relationships that structure a piece. Furthermore, the physical act of writing by hand, in itself, helps students not only process what they read, but remember it as well.

About the Passages

The 20 reproducible passages in this book, which vary in genres and forms, organizational structures, purposes, tones, and tasks, address six key reading-comprehension skills, from identifying main ideas and details, and sequencing events to separating facts from opinions and comparing and contrasting. Consult the table of contents to see the scope of skills, genres, forms, content areas, and Lexile scores of the passages. The Lexile scores fall within the ranges recommended for first graders. (The scores for grade 1, revised to reflect the more rigorous demands of today's higher standards, range from 190 to 420. This range addresses the variety commonly seen in typical first grade classrooms.)

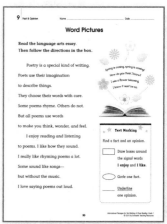

Each passage appears on its own page, beginning with the title, the genre or form of the passage, and the main comprehension skill the passage addresses. The passages include visual elements, such as photographs or diagrams, as well as typical text elements, such as boldface type and captions.

The passages are organized to help scaffold young students' understanding of each comprehension skill. For example, in the first passage of the fact and opinion section, students identify one fact and a signal word phrase. The next passage has them identify one opinion and a signal word phrase. In the final two passages, they practice identifying facts and opinions, as well as pertinent signal words and phrases.

Until your students are reading independently, the passages will work best as shared reading activities using an interactive whiteboard or document camera, or during guided reading so that you can scaffold and support readers. (See the next page for a close-reading routine to model for students.)

Reading-Comprehension Question Pages

Following each passage is a reproducible "Do More" page of text-dependent comprehension questions: two are multiple-choice questions that call for a single response and a brief, text-based explanation to justify that choice. The other is an open-response item. The questions address a range of comprehension strategies and skills. All questions share the goal of ensuring that students engage in close reading of the text, grasp its key ideas, and provide text-based evidence to support their answers. Have additional paper on hand so students have ample space to write complete and thorough answers.

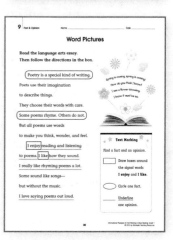

An answer key (pages 54–63) includes annotated versions of each marked passage and sample answers to its related questions. Maintain flexibility in assessing student responses, as some markings and answers to open-response questions may vary. (And because students are likely to mark different places in the text as examples for particular skills, the annotated versions in the answer key highlight a variety of possible responses.) Encourage students to self-assess and revise their answers as you review the text markings together. This approach encourages discussion, comparison, extension, reinforcement, and correlation to other reading skills.

Teaching Routine for Close Reading and Purposeful Text Marking

Any text can become more accessible to readers once they have learned to bring various strategies, such as purposeful text marking, to the reading process. Here is one suggested routine that may be effective in your classroom.

Preview

- **Engage prior knowledge** of the topic of the piece and its genre. Help students link it to similar topics or examples of the genre they may have read.

- **Identify the reading skill** for which students will be marking the text. Display or distribute the Comprehension Skill Summary Card that applies to the passage. Go over its key ideas. (See Comprehension Skill Summary Cards, page 8, for more.)

Model *(for the first passage, to familiarize students with the process)*

- **Display the passage**, using an interactive whiteboard, document camera, or other resource, and provide students with their own copy. Preview the text with students by having them read the title and look at any photographs, diagrams, or other graphic elements.

- **Draw attention to the markings** students will use to enhance their understanding of the piece. Link the text marking box to the Comprehension Skill Summary Card for clarification.

- **Read aloud the passage** as students follow along. Guide students to think about the skill and to note any questions they may have on sticky-notes.

- **Mark the text together.** Begin by numbering the paragraphs. Then discuss the choices you make when marking the text, demonstrating and explaining how the various text elements support the skill. Check that students understand how to mark the text using the various icons and graphics shown in the text marking box.

Read

- **Display each passage for a shared reading experience.** Do a quick-read of the passage together to familiarize students with it. Then read it together a second time, pausing as necessary to answer questions, draw connections, or clarify words as needed. Then read the passage once more, this time with an eye to the text features described in the text marking box.

- **Invite students to offer ideas for additional markings.** These might include noting unfamiliar vocabulary, an idiom or phrase they may not understand, or an especially interesting, unusual, or important detail they want to remember. Model how to use sticky-notes, colored pencils, highlighters, question marks, or check marks.

Respond

- **If students are able, have them read the passage independently.** This reading is intended to allow students to mark the text themselves, with your support, as needed. It will also prepare them to discuss the piece and offer their views about it.

- **Have students answer the questions** on the companion Do More page. Depending on the abilities of your students, you might read aloud the questions, and then have them answer orally. Model how to look back at the text markings and other text evidence for assistance. This will help students provide complete and supported responses.

Informational Passages for Text Marking & Close Reading: Grade 1
© 2015 by Scholastic Teaching Resources

Comprehension Skill Summary Cards

To help students review the six reading-comprehension skills this book addresses and the specific terms associated with each, have them use the six reproducible Comprehension Skill Summary Cards (pages 10–12). The boldface terms on each card are the same ones students will identify as they mark the text.

You might duplicate, cut out, and distribute a particular Comprehension Skill Summary Card before assigning a passage that focuses on that skill. Discuss the elements of the skill together to ensure that students fully grasp it. Encourage students to save and collect the cards, which they can use as a set of reading aids to refer to whenever they read any type of informational text. Or display the cards in a reading center in your classroom, where they will be available at all times.

Tips and Suggestions

- The text-marking process is versatile and adaptable. While numbering, boxing, circling, and underlining are the most common methods, you can personalize the strategy for your class if it helps augment the process. You might have students use letters to mark text; they can, for example, write MI to indicate a main idea, D to mark a detail, or F for fact and O for opinion. Whichever technique you use, focus on the need for consistency of marking.

- You may wish to extend the text-marking strategy by having students identify other aspects of writing, such as confusing words, expressions, or idioms. Moreover, you can invite students to write their own notes and questions on sticky-notes.

Comprehension Skill

Main Idea & Details

You read to find out things. Some things are more important than others.

- The **main idea** answers the question "Who (or What) is this about?"

- The **main idea** is the most important point in the paragraph. Look for a sentence that tells the main idea.

- **Details** add facts about the main idea. Details tell more about the main idea.

Comprehension Skill

Sequence of Events

When you read, look for the **order** in which things happen.

- **Events** are actions, steps, or things that happen.

- The **sequence** is the order of the events.

- **Signal words** give clues about the sequence of events.

  Examples: **first, second, next, then, now, later, after,** and **finally**.

Comprehension Skill

Compare & Contrast

When you read, think about how people, things, or ideas are **alike**. Also think about how they are **different**.

- To **compare** means to tell how things are the same or alike.

- To **contrast** means to tell how things are different.

- **Signal words** give clues that help you compare and contrast.

  Examples for comparing: **both, too, like,** and **also**.

  Examples for contrasting: **but, only, unlike,** and **different**.

Informational Passages for Text Marking & Close Reading: Grade 1
© 2015 by Scholastic Teaching Resources

Connections to the Standards

The lessons in this book support the College and Career Readiness Anchor Standards for Reading for students in grades K–12. These broad standards, which serve as the basis of many state standards, were developed to establish rigorous educational expectations with the goal of providing students nationwide with a quality education that prepares them for college and careers. The chart below details how the lessons align with specific reading standards for informational text for students in grade 1.

These materials also address language standards, including skills in the conventions of standard English, knowledge of language, and vocabulary acquisition and use. In addition, students meet writing standards as they answer questions about the passages, demonstrating their ability to convey ideas coherently, clearly, and with support from the text.

Key Ideas and Details

- Ask and answer questions about key details in a text.

- Identify the main topic and retell key details of a text.

- Describe the connection between two individuals, events, ideas, or pieces of information in a text.

Craft and Structure

- Ask and answer questions to help determine or clarify the meaning of words and phrases in a text.

- Know and use various text features (e.g., headings, tables of contents, glossaries, electronic menus, icons) to locate key facts or information in a text.

- Distinguish between information provided by pictures or other illustrations and information provided by the words in a text.

Integration of Knowledge and Ideas

- Use the illustrations and details in a text to describe its key ideas.

- Identify the reasons an author gives to support points in a text.

Range of Reading and Level of Text Complexity

- With prompting and support, read informational texts appropriately complex for grade 1.

Source: © Copyright 2010 National Governors Association Center for Best Practices and Council of Chief State School Officers. All rights reserved.

Sequence of Events

When you read, look for the **order** in which things happen.

- **Events** are actions, steps, or things that happen.

- The **sequence** is the order of the events.

- **Signal words** give clues about the sequence of events.

Examples: **first, second, next, then, now, later, after,** and **finally**.

Main Idea & Details

You read to find out things. Some things are more important than others.

- The **main idea** answers the question "Who (or What) is this about?"

- The **main idea** is the most important point in the paragraph. Look for a sentence that tells the main idea.

- **Details** add facts about the main idea. Details tell more about the main idea.

Informational Passages for Text Marking & Close Reading: Grade 1
© 2015 by Scholastic Teaching Resources

Compare & Contrast

When you read, think about how people, things, or ideas are **alike.** Also think about how they are **different.**

- To **compare** means to tell how things are the same or alike.

- To **contrast** means to tell how things are different.

- **Signal words** give clues that help you compare and contrast.

  Examples for comparing: **both, too, like,** and **also.**

  Examples for contrasting: **but, only, unlike,** and **different.**

Fact & Opinion

When you read, try to spot and separate **facts** from **opinions.**

- A **fact** is a statement you can prove. Facts are true.

- An **opinion** tells what someone believes or feels. Opinions vary because people have different beliefs or feelings.

- **Signal words** give clues that help you tell facts from opinions.

  Examples for facts: **know,** and **found out.**

  Examples for opinions: **believe, like, think, agree, disagree, love,** and **feel.**

Informational Passages for Text Marking & Close Reading: Grade 1

Problem & Solution

Sometimes you will read about **problems** and how they get **solved.**

- A **problem** is a kind of trouble or puzzle. A problem needs to be fixed or solved.

- A **solution** is how to solve a problem. A solution makes things better.

- **Signal words** give clues to a problem and its solutions.

Examples for problems: **question, need,** and **trouble.**

Examples for solutions: **answer, fix, idea, plan, result,** and **solve.**

Cause & Effect

When you read, think about why something happens. Also think about what happens because of it.

- A **cause** is why something happens.

- An **effect** is what happens.

- If you know the **cause,** try to understand the **effect.**

- If you know the **effect,** try to figure out the **cause.**

- **Signal words** give clues that link a cause and its effect.

Examples: **because, since, so,** and **result.**

12

Informational
Text Passages

Name _____   Date _____

Thumbs Up!

Read the article about the human body.
Then follow the directions in the box.

Thumbs are special fingers.

All your fingers can move in and out.

All can move from side to side.

All can bend and wiggle.

All can move in a circle.

But only a thumb can touch

every other fingertip.

No other fingers can meet like this.

Try it.

Your thumbs help you grab

and hold things.

Can you pick up a penny

without using your thumb?

Text Marking

Find the main idea.
Find one detail.

⬭ Circle the main idea.

_____ Underline a detail.

Name _____ Date _____

Thumbs Up!

▶ **Answer each question. Use the article and photo.**

1 Which is something ONLY thumbs can do?

○ A. bend and wiggle

○ B. move in a circle

○ C. touch every other fingertip

What helped you answer? _____

_____

_____

2 What do your thumbs help you do?

○ A. wiggle   ○ B. pick things up   ○ C. count pennies

What helped you answer? _____

_____

_____

3 Try to pick up a penny without using your thumb.
What happens? Write about it.

_____

_____

_____

_____

Name _____ Date _____

Children's Day in Japan

Read the culture article.
Then follow the directions in the box.

Japan has a special holiday

every May 5. It is just for kids.

It is called Children's Day.

This holiday is joyful.

Families spend the day together.

They honor their children.

They wish for them to be healthy

and happy.

Fish flags wave in the air.

Kids play games.

They eat treats like sweet rice cakes.

Fish flags

Text Marking

Find the main idea.
Find two details.

◯ Circle the main idea.

___ Underline
two details.

Informational Passages for Text Marking & Close Reading: Grade 1
© 2015 by Scholastic Teaching Resources

Name _____ Date _____

Children's Day in Japan

▶ **Answer each question. Use the article and photo.**

1 Which happens on Children's Day in Japan?

   ○ A. It is a day to be sad.

   ○ B. Children visit parents at work.

   ○ C. Fish flags wave in the air.

   What helped you answer? _____

   _____

2 What is a favorite food on Children's Day?

   ○ A. fish cakes   ○ B. rice cakes   ○ C. tea cakes

   What helped you answer? _____

   _____

3 What happens in Japan on May 5? Write about it.

   _____

   _____

   _____

   _____

   _____

   _____

Informational Passages for Text Marking & Close Reading: Grade 1

Name _____ Date _____

Here Comes a Parade!

Read the entertainment article.
Then follow the directions in the box.

Parades are great fun to watch.

Balloons and banners fly.

Bands play lively music.

Crowds wave at the people marching.

The marchers wear colorful costumes.

Some parades have live animals.

Others have silly clowns.

Many parades have large floats.

Floats are like stages that roll along.

Sometimes famous people ride on them.

Would you like to march in a parade?

Parade float

⭐ **Text Marking** ⭐

Find the main idea.

Find three details.

◯ Circle the main idea.

_____ Underline
three details.

Informational Passages for Text Marking & Close Reading: Grade 1
© 2015 by Scholastic Teaching Resources

Here Comes a Parade!

▶ **Answer each question. Use the article and photo.**

1 What makes a parade fun to watch?

   ○ A. There are colorful costumes and happy music.

   ○ B. There are no crowds.

   ○ C. There is peace and quiet.

What helped you answer? _____

_____

_____

2 Which is NOT true about floats?

   ○ A. They can be big.

   ○ B. They stay in one place.

   ○ C. They are like moving stages.

What helped you answer? _____

_____

_____

3 Look at the photo. Tell what it is. Describe what you see.

_____

_____

_____

_____

Serving Star Fruit

Read the food article.

Then follow the directions in the box.

Did you ever see a star fruit?

It is yellow-green inside and out.

Star fruit tastes good.

And it is fun to serve.

Here is what to do.

First, wash the star fruit.

Next, lay the star fruit on a cutting board.

Then, ask a grown-up to cut thin slices.

What shape do the slices have?

> ### Text Marking
>
> Find the sequence of steps for serving star fruit.
>
> ☐ Draw boxes around the signal words **first**, **next**, and **then**.
>
> ___ <u>Underline</u> three steps.
>
> 1-2-3 Number the steps in order.

Whole star fruit

Sliced star fruit

Informational Passages for Text Marking & Close Reading: Grade 1
© 2015 by Scholastic Teaching Resources

Name _____ Date _____

Serving Star Fruit

▶ **Answer each question. Use the article and photos.**

1 What color is a star fruit?

○ A. white   ○ B. yellow-green   ○ C. cannot tell

What helped you answer? _____

_____

_____

2 What is the second thing you do to serve star fruit?

○ A. Wash the star fruit.

○ B. Peel the star fruit.

○ C. Put the star fruit on a cutting board.

What helped you answer? _____

_____

_____

3 Why is star fruit fun to serve?

_____

_____

_____

_____

Informational Passages for Text Marking & Close Reading: Grade 1
© 2015 by Scholastic Teaching Resources

Guests at a Ranch

Read the letter.
Then follow the directions in the box.

A photo of the ranch

Hi Grandpa,

We had a great time visiting

a working ranch for three days.

You would have loved it!

Here is what we did.

First, we met the owners.

They wore real cowboy boots and hats!

Then, we went to see the guest barn.

That is where we would sleep.

But we were too excited to rest.

So, next we got to meet Blue and Scout.

We rode them every day!

Love, Benjy

Text Marking

Find the sequence of events for the ranch visit.

▢ Draw boxes around the signal words **first**, **then**, and **next**.

___ Underline three events.

1-2-3 Number the events in order.

Name _____ Date _____

Guests at a Ranch

▶ **Answer each question. Use the letter and photo.**

1 What did Benjy notice about the owners?

○ A. They were full of mud.

○ B. They wore cowboy boots.

○ C. They were tall and strong.

What helped you answer? _____

_____

_____

_____

2 Who are Blue and Scout?

○ A. They are horses. ○ B. They are helpers. ○ C. They are owners.

What helped you answer? _____

_____

_____

_____

3 Why do you think Benjy was too excited to rest?

_____

_____

_____

_____

_____

Informational Passages for Text Marking & Close Reading: Grade 1
© 2015 by Scholastic Teaching Resources

A Living Museum

Read the museum review.

Then follow the directions in the box.

A **botanic** (buh-TAN-ik) **garden**

is a living museum.

We visited one today.

We saw all kinds of plants

and flowers inside

a big glass building.

First, we visited the rain forest room.

Those plants were very tall and had

giant leaves. I touched a huge fern.

Next came the rose room.

What pretty colors!

The cactus room was the last part

of the garden we saw.

We looked, but did not touch!

This glass building
is called a **greenhouse**.

⭐ Text Marking ⭐

Find the sequence of events
for the garden visit.

☐	Draw boxes around the signal words **first**, **next**, and **last**.
_____	Underline three events.
1-2-3	Number the events in order.

Informational Passages for Text Marking & Close Reading: Grade 1
© 2015 by Scholastic Teaching Resources

Name _____ Date _____

A Living Museum

▶ **Answer each question. Use the review and photos.**

1 Which belongs in a botanic garden?

○ A. paintings   ○ B. animals   ○ C. plants

What helped you answer? _____

_____

_____

2 Which room of the garden did the writer visit last?

○ A. the rose room   ○ B. the cactus room   ○ C. the rain forest room

What helped you answer? _____

_____

_____

3 Look at the photos.
Why is a botanic garden building made of glass?

_____

_____

_____

_____

About a Scooter

Read the description.
Then follow the directions in the box.

Today I measured my new scooter.

Here is what I found out.

First, I measured the **deck**.

That is the part you stand on.

It is 25 inches long.

It is 12 inches wide.

Then I measured all three wheels.

The front wheel is 6 inches across.

Each back wheel is 5 inches across.

The handlebars are easy to grip.

I think this is the best scooter ever!

Text Marking

☐ Draw a box around the signal words **found out**.

⬭ Circle one fact.

Informational Passages for Text Marking & Close Reading: Grade 1
© 2015 by Scholastic Teaching Resources

Name _____ Date _____

About a Scooter

▶ **Answer each question. Use the description and photo.**

1 How do you use the **deck** of a scooter?

○ A. You stand on it.   ○ B. You grip it.   ○ C. You paint it.

What helped you answer? _____

_____

_____

2 Which word goes with a fact?

○ A. best   ○ B. inches   ○ C. easy

What helped you answer? _____

_____

_____

3 How do you know that the last sentence is NOT a fact?

_____

_____

_____

_____

_____

Name _____ Date _____

Around the Edges

Read the nutrition article.

Then follow the directions in the box.

The outside of bread is hard and brown.

This part is the **crust**.

Scientists know that the crust

is good for you. It is full of fiber

and other healthy things.

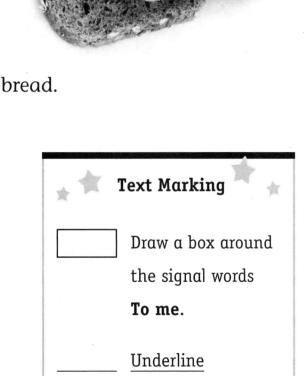

Many kids do not like the crust.

They say the crust is the worst part of bread.

But I do not agree.

I love the crust. I like that it is chewy.

To me, it makes a neat border

for the bread.

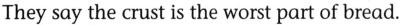

★ Text Marking ★

☐ Draw a box around the signal words **To me.**

___ Underline one opinion.

Informational Passages for Text Marking & Close Reading: Grade 1
© 2015 by Scholastic Teaching Resources

Name _____ Date _____

Around the Edges

▶ **Answer each question. Use the article and photo.**

1 Which words best describe a bread **crust**?

○ A. soft and chewy

○ B. hard and brown

○ C. brown and full of seeds

What helped you answer? _____

_____

_____

2 What is the writer's opinion of the crust on bread?

○ A. It tastes bad.

○ B. It is the same as the rest of the bread.

○ C. It is nice and chewy.

What helped you answer? _____

_____

_____

3 What would a scientist tell you about eating the crust on bread?

_____

_____

_____

_____

Informational Passages for Text Marking & Close Reading: Grade 1
© 2015 by Scholastic Teaching Resources

Name _____ Date _____

Word Pictures

Read the language arts essay.
Then follow the directions in the box.

Poetry is a special kind of writing.

Poets use their imagination

to describe things.

They choose their words with care.

Some poems rhyme. Others do not.

But all poems use words

to make you think, wonder, and feel.

I enjoy reading and listening

to poems. I like how they sound.

I really like rhyming poems a lot.

Some sound like songs—

but without the music.

I love saying poems out loud.

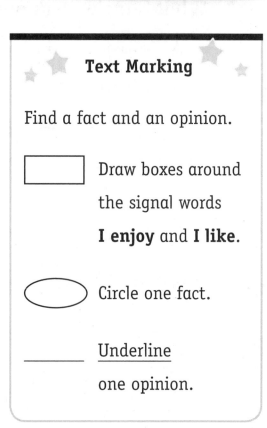

Spring is coming, spring is coming!
How do you think I know?
I see a flower blooming.
I know it must be so.

Text Marking

Find a fact and an opinion.

☐ Draw boxes around
the signal words
I enjoy and **I like**.

◯ Circle one fact.

___ Underline
one opinion.

Name _____ Date _____

Word Pictures

▶ **Answer each question. Use the essay and picture.**

1 Which is TRUE about all poems?

○ A. They are a special kind of writing.

○ B. They sound like songs.

○ C. They always rhyme.

What helped you answer? _____

_____

_____

2 What about poems does the writer enjoy a lot?

○ A. writing them

○ B. listening for the rhymes

○ C. how short they are

What helped you answer? _____

_____

_____

3 The title of this essay is "Word Pictures."
What do you think this means?

_____

_____

_____

_____

_____

Informational Passages for Text Marking & Close Reading: Grade 1
© 2015 by Scholastic Teaching Resources

Name _____ Date _____

Into the Water

Read the sports article.

Then follow the directions in the box.

Can you use your arms and legs

to move yourself through water?

If so, then you can swim.

And did you know that swimming

exercises the whole body?

It makes you strong and can

keep you safe.

My aunt taught me to swim.

She believed it was a wise idea.

I was little and felt scared at first.

But I learned and now I really love it.

I would swim every day if I could.

Learning to swim

Text Marking

Find the facts and opinions.

☐ Draw boxes around the signal words **know**, **believed**, and **felt**.

◯ Circle two facts.

___ Underline two opinions.

Name _____   Date _____

Into the Water

▶ **Answer each question. Use the article and photo.**

1 What does the writer now think about swimming?

○ A. It is scary.

○ B. It is too hard to learn.

○ C. It is something to do every day, if possible.

What helped you answer? _____

_____

_____

2 Why is swimming good for you?

○ A. It makes you strong.

○ B. It cools you off.

○ C. It is easy to learn.

What helped you answer? _____

_____

_____

_____

3 Describe what it means to swim.

_____

_____

_____

_____

Name _____ Date _____

Two Small Drums

Read the music article.

Then follow the directions in the box.

Tambourine

A **tambourine** (tam-buh-REEN)

is a small drum. You hold it in your hand.

A **tom-tom** is another small drum.

Look at the pictures.

Both drums are round.

You can tap or hit both of them.

Both make thumping sounds.

But a tambourine has metal circles

around the sides. It can thump.

And it can also jingle.

Tom-tom

⭐ Text Marking ⭐

Compare a tambourine
and a tom-tom.

☐ Draw a box around
the signal word
both.

◯ Circle one way
they are alike.

Informational Passages for Text Marking & Close Reading: Grade 1
© 2015 by Scholastic Teaching Resources

Name _____ Date _____

Two Small Drums

▶ **Answer each question. Use the article and photos.**

1 This article compares _____.

    ○ A. drums and bells

    ○ B. two kinds of drums

    ○ C. thumps and jingles

What helped you answer? _____

_____

_____

2 Which is a way that tambourines are NOT like tom-toms?

    ○ A. They can jingle.   ○ B. They are bigger.   ○ C. They are round.

What helped you answer? _____

_____

_____

3 Look at the photos. Which drum is played with sticks?
Write how you can tell.

_____

_____

_____

_____

Informational Passages for Text Marking & Close Reading: Grade 1
© 2015 by Scholastic Teaching Resources

Name _____ Date _____

Two Ways to Fly

Read the transportation article.
Then follow the directions in the box.

Both **airplanes** and **gliders**

fly in the sky. Both have wings.

Both have pilots. But they are different

in a very important way.

Airplanes have engines, but gliders do not.

So how do gliders fly?

An airplane pulls a glider into the air.

They go higher and higher together.

Then the airplane lets go. The glider floats alone.

The pilot guides it home. It lands safely.

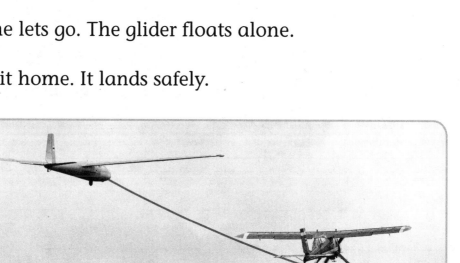

An airplane towing a glider with a rope

Informational Passages for Text Marking & Close Reading: Grade 1
© 2015 by Scholastic Teaching Resources

Two Ways to Fly

▶ **Answer each question. Use the article and photo.**

1 Which is a way that airplanes and gliders are ALIKE?

○ A. Both have pilots.

○ B. Both have engines.

○ C. Both get pulled up into the air.

What helped you answer? _____

_____

_____

2 Why does a glider need to be pulled into the air?

○ A. Its wings are too long.

○ B. It doesn't have a pilot.

○ C. It does not have an engine to power it.

What helped you answer? _____

_____

_____

3 Airplanes can fly farther than gliders can.
Why do you think this is so?

_____

_____

_____

_____

Informational Passages for Text Marking & Close Reading: Grade 1
© 2015 by Scholastic Teaching Resources

Which Insect Is It?

Read the article about insects.
Then follow the directions in the box.

Is it a **butterfly**? Or is it a **moth**?

Both kinds of insects are colorful.

Most butterflies have bright colors.

Moths have pale colors.

Butterflies and moths need

to keep warm. But they keep warm

in different ways.

A butterfly warms itself in the sun.

A moth warms up by moving its wings.

Both insects fly.

Butterflies fly in the day.

But moths fly at night.

Butterfly

Moth

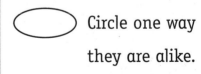

Text Marking

Compare and contrast
butterflies and moths.

☐ Draw boxes around
the signal words
both, **but**,
and **different**.

◯ Circle one way
they are alike.

___ Underline one way
they are different.

Informational Passages for Text Marking & Close Reading: Grade 1
© 2015 by Scholastic Teaching Resources

Name _____ Date _____

Which Insect Is It?

▶ **Answer each question. Use the article and photos.**

1 This article compares and contrasts _____.

○ A. day and night

○ B. moths and butterflies

○ C. flying and resting

What helped you answer? _____

_____

2 What does a moth do to stay warm?

○ A. It rests in the sun.

○ B. It flaps its wings.

○ C. It sleeps under its wings.

What helped you answer? _____

_____

3 What is another way that butterflies and moths are different?

_____

_____

_____

_____

Informational Passages for Text Marking & Close Reading: Grade 1
© 2015 by Scholastic Teaching Resources

Name _____ Date _____

Auks and Hawks

Read the article about birds.
Then follow the directions in the box.

Auks and **hawks** are birds.

Like all birds, both lay eggs.

Both fly and hunt.

In other ways, auks and hawks
are different. Auks are black and white.

Hawks come in many colors.

Auks have short legs with webbed feet.

Hawks have long, strong legs.

They have sharp claws.

Auks eat fish and other sea life.

Hawks eat small land animals, snakes,
and insects.

⭐ **Text Marking** ⭐

Compare and contrast
auks and hawks.

[☐] Draw boxes around
the signal words
like, **both**,
and **different**.

[◯] Circle two ways
they are alike.

[___] Underline two ways
they are different.

Informational Passages for Text Marking & Close Reading: Grade 1
© 2015 by Scholastic Teaching Resources

Name _____ Date _____

Auks and Hawks

▶ **Answer each question. Use the article and photos.**

1 This article compares and contrasts _____.

  ○ A. claws and webbed feet

  ○ B. birds and fish

  ○ C. hawks and auks

  What helped you answer? _____

  _____

  _____

2 Which is a way that auks and hawks are ALIKE?

  ○ A. Both eat snakes.

  ○ B. Both lay eggs.

  ○ C. Both have long legs.

  What helped you answer? _____

  _____

  _____

3 Look at the photos. Which is the hawk? Which is the auk? Write how you can tell.

  _____

  _____

  _____

Name _____ Date _____

High Waters

Read the earth science article.
Then follow the directions in the box.

A **flood** happens when water spills over.

What causes a flood?

Snow melts off mountains in the spring.

It turns into water.

The water runs downhill.

It flows into rivers.

Rainstorms add more water to rivers.

Rivers can't hold all that extra water.

So they **overflow**.

The water covers everything nearby.

Floods soak fields, roads, and towns.

A flooded home

★ Text Marking ★

Find the cause and effect
of a flood.

☐ Draw boxes around
the signal words
causes and **so**.

◯ Circle the cause.

___ Underline
the effect.

Informational Passages for Text Marking & Close Reading: Grade 1
© 2015 by Scholastic Teaching Resources

Name _____ Date _____

High Waters

▶ **Answer each question. Use the article and photo.**

1 The word **overflow** means _____.

○ A. heat up   ○ B. spill over   ○ C. get cold

What helped you answer? _____

_____

_____

2 Which does NOT cause floods?

○ A. rain   ○ B. melting snow   ○ C. fields and towns

What helped you answer? _____

_____

_____

3 Why do you think most floods happen in spring?

_____

_____

_____

_____

_____

_____

Informational Passages for Text Marking & Close Reading: Grade 1
© 2015 by Scholastic Teaching Resources

Name _____ Date _____

Ahhh . . . choo!

Read the health article.

Then follow the directions in the box.

Almost anything can cause a sneeze.

You might breathe in some dust,

cold air, or even pepper.

It tickles the inside of your nose.

So you need to clear it out.

Your brain gets the message.

It signals some muscles to get ready

to help. When they do, you suddenly feel

the results. Your eyes close tight.

Your mouth opens, and you sneeze:

AHHH . . . CHOO! The tickle is gone.

Text Marking

Find the cause and effects.

☐ Draw boxes around the signal words **cause** and **results**.

◯ Circle the cause.

___ Underline the effects.

Informational Passages for Text Marking & Close Reading: Grade 1

Name _____ Date _____

Ahhh . . . choo!

▶ **Answer each question. Use the article and photo.**

1 What does your brain do when your nose feels a tickle inside?

○ A. It sends messages to muscles that can help.

○ B. It removes dust from your nose.

○ C. It makes you feel sleepy.

What helped you answer? _____

_____

_____

2 Which is NOT an effect of having a tickle inside your nose?

○ A. You sneeze.

○ B. Your mouth opens.

○ C. You feel ticklish all over.

What helped you answer? _____

_____

_____

3 How does sneezing make you feel better?

_____

_____

_____

_____

Name _____ Date _____

A Little Big City

Read the social studies article.
Then follow the directions in the box.

New York is America's biggest city.

Many, many people live there.

Visitors and workers **pour in** daily.

But this busy city sits on a small piece

of land.

New York City is packed.

Everywhere you can see the effects

of too little space.

Buildings must rise high into the sky.

There are lots of shops.

But many are tiny.

Streets and sidewalks are narrow.

So crowds and traffic jams happen

every day.

A crowded New York City street

Text Marking

Find the cause and effects.

☐ Draw boxes around the signal words **effects** and **so**.

◯ Circle the cause.

___ Underline two effects.

Informational Passages for Text Marking & Close Reading: Grade 1
© 2015 by Scholastic Teaching Resources

Name _____ Date _____

A Little Big City

▶ **Answer each question. Use the article and photo.**

1 Which is a CAUSE of crowds in New York City?

○ A. traffic jams   ○ B. tall buildings   ○ C. too little space

What helped you answer? _____

_____

_____

_____

2 Which means the same as **pour in**?

○ A. ride boats to the city

○ B. come in many at a time

○ C. bring along something to drink

What helped you answer? _____

_____

_____

_____

3 How can New York be a big city if it doesn't have much land?

_____

_____

_____

_____

_____

Name _____ Date _____

Pool Hero

Read the news article.

Then follow the directions in the box.

Riley Braden, age five, was swimming

in a hotel pool in Florida. She noticed

a baby all alone at the steps. **Kerplash!**

The baby slipped into the water and sank.

What a problem!

Riley knew she had to help.

She took a deep breath.

She dove down and grabbed the child.

She pulled her up, shouting,

"I've got the baby! I've got the baby!"

Riley at the pool

★ ★ **Text Marking** ★ ★

Find the problem
and the solution.

☐ Draw boxes around
the signal words
problem and **help**.

◯ Circle the problem.

_____ Underline
the solution.

Informational Passages for Text Marking & Close Reading: Grade 1
© 2015 by Scholastic Teaching Resources

Name _____ Date _____

Pool Hero

▶ **Answer each question. Use the article and photo.**

1 The writer uses **Kerplash!** for the sound of _____.

○ A. crying　　　○ B. splashing　　　○ C. laughing

What helped you answer? _____

_____

_____

_____

2 How did Riley know she had to help?

○ A. Riley liked to swim.

○ B. Riley knew the baby.

○ C. Riley thought the baby might drown.

What helped you answer? _____

_____

_____

_____

3 Why do you think Riley shouted the same words two times?

_____

_____

_____

_____

_____

Informational Passages for Text Marking & Close Reading: Grade 1
© 2015 by Scholastic Teaching Resources

Latino Life in *Libros*

Read the author study.
Then follow the directions in the box.

Lulu Delacre (De-LAK-ray)

speaks Spanish and English.

So does her family. Lulu looked

for interesting books to read

with her children. But she found

a problem. There were very few books

about Latino people.

Delacre got an idea.

She would write her own books.

She wrote about families like hers.

She shared Latino stories, songs,

and ways of life. Her solution worked.

She has become a famous author.

Author Lulu Delacre

Libros is the Spanish word for "books."

Text Marking

Find the problem
and the solution.

☐ Draw boxes around
the signal words
problem, **idea**,
and **solution**.

◯ Circle the problem.

___ Underline
the solution.

Name _____ Date _____

Latino Life in *Libros*

▶ **Answer each question. Use the author study and photo.**

1 Which is TRUE about Lulu Delacre?

○ A. She speaks only Spanish.

○ B. She speaks only English.

○ C. She speaks English and Spanish.

What helped you answer? _____

_____

_____

2 What does Lulu Delacre mostly write about?

○ A. Latino people and ways of life

○ B. famous authors

○ C. children

What helped you answer? _____

_____

_____

3 Why did Lulu Delacre decide to write her own books?

_____

_____

_____

_____

Informational Passages for Text Marking & Close Reading: Grade 1

Name _____ Date _____

Keeping Cool

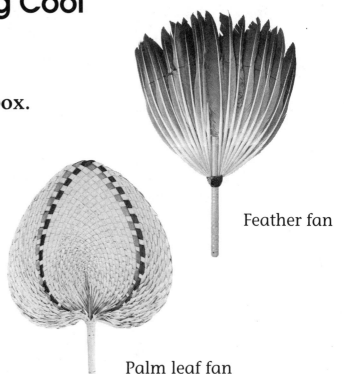

Feather fan

Read the social studies article.

Then follow the directions in the box.

How can we cool off?

People who live in hot places

have always had this problem.

One simple answer was to stay

out of the sun.

People sat under shady trees.

They rested in cool caves.

A second solution was to make air

move faster. Someone invented

the hand fan. A person might flap

a big leaf back and forth.

This made a breeze.

People have been using this simple tool

ever since.

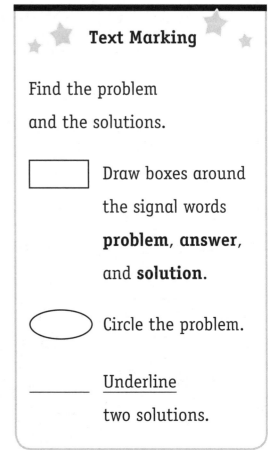

Palm leaf fan

⭐ Text Marking ⭐

Find the problem
and the solutions.

☐ Draw boxes around
the signal words
problem, **answer**,
and **solution**.

◯ Circle the problem.

___ Underline
two solutions.

Informational Passages for Text Marking & Close Reading: Grade 1
© 2015 by Scholastic Teaching Resources

Name _____ Date _____

Keeping Cool

▶ **Answer each question. Use the article and photos.**

1 Why would people rest in caves?

○ A. Caves made good hiding places.

○ B. It was cooler inside a cave.

○ C. It was warmer inside a cave.

What helped you answer? _____

_____

_____

2 How does a hand fan work?

○ A. You flap it to make a breeze.

○ B. It uses batteries.

○ C. It plugs into the wall.

What helped you answer? _____

_____

_____

3 Look at the photos of the fans. How are they alike?

_____

_____

_____

_____

Informational Passages for Text Marking & Close Reading: Grade 1

Answer Key

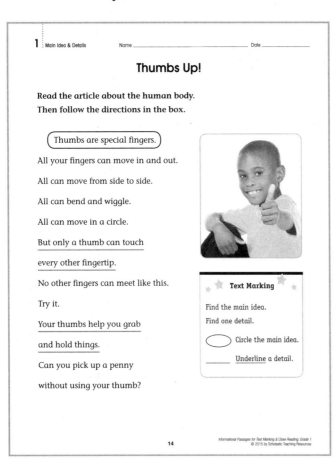

Passage 1: Thumbs Up!

1. C; Sample answer: It says in the sixth sentence that only thumbs can do this.

2. B; Sample answer: The article says that this is something thumbs help you do.

3. Sample answers: It was really hard to grab the penny without using my thumb.

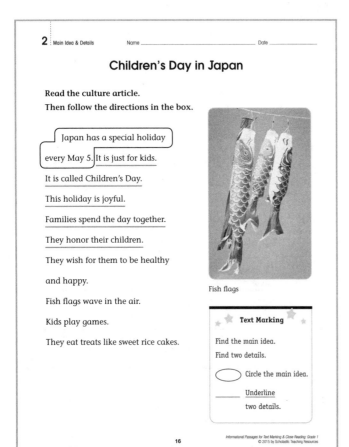

Passage 2: Children's Day in Japan

1. C; Sample answer: The article says that fish flags wave in the air. It doesn't talk about the other things.

2. B; Sample answer: This is the only food the article talks about.

3. Sample answers: It is a family holiday. Kids eat sweets, play games, and spend the day with their families.

Sample Text Markings

3 Main Idea & Details   Name _____ Date _____

Here Comes a Parade!

Read the entertainment article.
Then follow the directions in the box.

(Parades are great fun to watch.)

Balloons and banners fly.

Bands play lively music.

Crowds wave at the people marching.

The marchers wear colorful costumes.

Some parades have live animals.

Others have silly clowns.

Many parades have large floats.

Floats are like stages that roll along.

Sometimes famous people ride on them.

Would you like to march in a parade?

Parade float

Text Marking

Find the main idea.
Find three details.

⬭   Circle the main idea.

_____   Underline
three details.

18

Informational Passages for Text Marking & Close Reading: Grade 1
© 2015 by Scholastic Teaching Resources

◀ Sample Text Markings

Passage 3: Here Comes a Parade!

1. A; Sample answer: I picked A because it says so in the article.

2. B; Sample answer: This is the only answer that is not true. The article says that floats roll along.

3. Sample answers: I see a big parade float going down a street. It has clocks on it and a tower like in a castle. There are people riding on the float. Others are watching from the sides.

---

4 Sequence of Events   Name _____ Date _____

Serving Star Fruit

Read the food article.
Then follow the directions in the box.

Did you ever see a star fruit?

It is yellow-green inside and out.

Star fruit tastes good.

And it is fun to serve.

Here is what to do.

(1) | First, | wash the star fruit.

(2) | Next, | lay the star fruit on a cutting board.

(3) | Then, | ask a grown-up to cut thin slices.

What shape do the slices have?

Text Marking

Find the sequence of steps
for serving star fruit.

☐   Draw boxes around
the signal words
first, **next**,
and **then**.

_____   Underline
three steps.

1-2-3   Number the steps
in order.

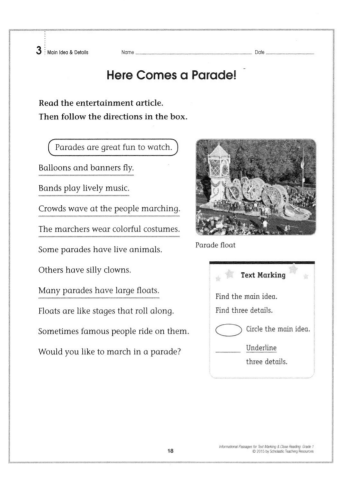

Whole star fruit   Sliced star fruit

20

Informational Passages for Text Marking & Close Reading: Grade 1
© 2015 by Scholastic Teaching Resources

◀ Sample Text Markings

Passage 4: Serving Star Fruit

1. B; Sample answer: It says that star fruit is yellow-green in the second sentence.

2. C; Sample answer: The second step says to lay the star fruit on a cutting board.

3. Sample answer: Each slice looks like a little star that you can eat.

Passage 5: Guests at a Ranch

1. B; Sample answer: I picked B because I read that in the fifth sentence.

2. A; The letter says that Benjy rode them. So I think they must be the names of horses on the ranch.

3. Sample answer: I bet Benjy couldn't wait to meet the horses and maybe see more of the ranch.

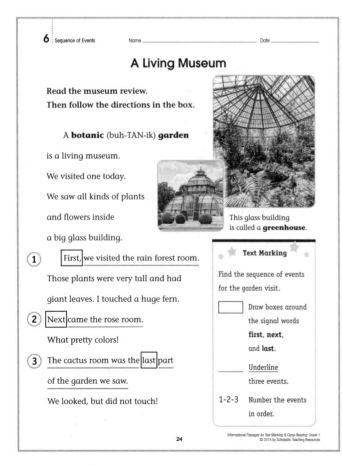

Passage 6: A Living Museum

1. C; Sample answer: I picked C because I read this in the first paragraph.

2. B; Sample answer: The writer says the cactus room was the last part of the garden they saw.

3. Sample answer: I think this is to let the sunlight shine on the plants to keep them alive.

7 Fact & Opinion   Name _____   Date _____

About a Scooter

Read the description.
Then follow the directions in the box.

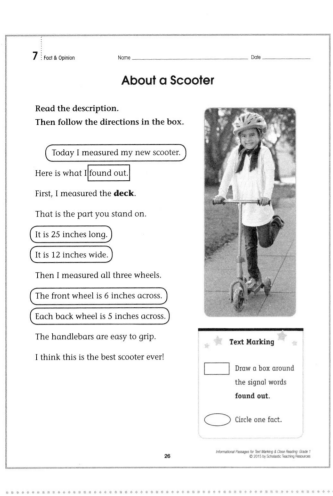

Today I measured my new scooter.

Here is what I found out.

First, I measured the **deck**.

That is the part you stand on.

It is 25 inches long.

It is 12 inches wide.

Then I measured all three wheels.

The front wheel is 6 inches across.

Each back wheel is 5 inches across.

The handlebars are easy to grip.

I think this is the best scooter ever!

Text Marking

☐ Draw a box around the signal words **found out**.

⬭ Circle one fact.

26

Passage 7: About a Scooter

1. A; Sample answer: In the fourth sentence, it says you stand on the deck.

2. B; Sample answer: You can measure inches with a ruler, so the number of inches is a fact.

3. Sample answer: I think it is an opinion because the writer says "I think."

---

8 Fact & Opinion   Name _____   Date _____

Around the Edges

Read the nutrition article.
Then follow the directions in the box.

The outside of bread is hard and brown.

This part is the **crust**.

Scientists know that the crust

is good for you. It is full of fiber

and other healthy things.

Many kids do not like the crust.

They say the crust is the worst part of bread.

But I do not agree.

I love the crust. I like that it is chewy.

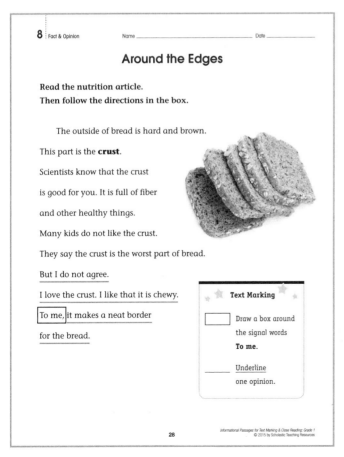

To me, it makes a neat border

for the bread.

Text Marking

☐ Draw a box around the signal words **To me**.

___ Underline one opinion.

28

Passage 8: Around the Edges

1. B; Sample answer: This is what it says in the first sentence.

2. C; Sample answer: I picked C because the writer tells us that.

3. Sample answer: I think a scientist would tell me to eat the crust because it is good and healthy for me.

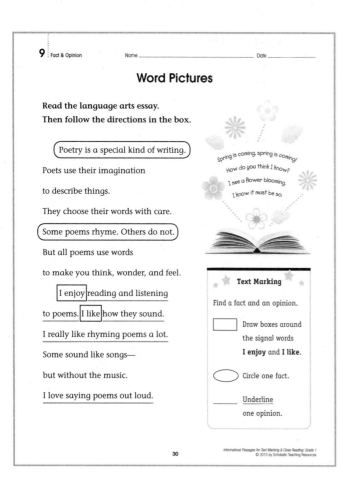

Passage 9: Word Pictures

1. A; Sample answer: I picked A because not all poems sound like songs, not all poems rhyme, and the essay says poetry is a special kind of writing.

2. B; Sample answer: I picked B because the writer says so in the second paragraph.

3. Sample answer: I think that poets carefully pick words that help readers see pictures in their minds.

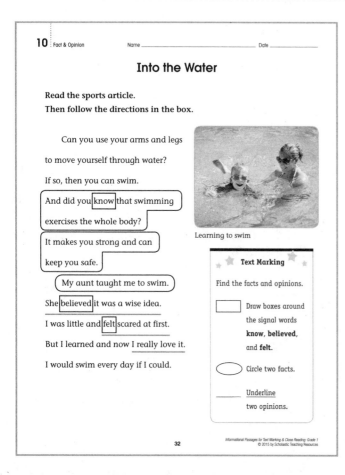

Passage 10: Into the Water

1. C; Sample answer: The writer says this in the last sentence.

2. A; Sample answer: I read that swimming makes you strong in the first paragraph.

3. Sample answer: Swimming means you use your arms and legs to move yourself through water.

Informational Passages for Text Marking & Close Reading: Grade 1
© 2015 by Scholastic Teaching Resources

Passage 11: Two Small Drums

1. B; Sample answer: The article compares two kinds of drums—a tambourine and a tom-tom.

2. A; Sample answer: The article says that a tambourine can jingle. This is the main way tambourines are different from tom-toms.

3. Sample answer: The tom-tom is on the bottom. It shows two sticks resting on it.

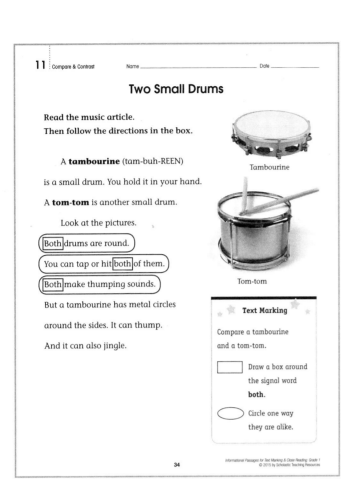

11 Compare & Contrast   Name _____   Date _____

Two Small Drums

Read the music article.
Then follow the directions in the box.

A **tambourine** (tam-buh-REEN)

is a small drum. You hold it in your hand.

A **tom-tom** is another small drum.

Look at the pictures.

Both drums are round.

You can tap or hit both of them.

Both make thumping sounds.

But a tambourine has metal circles

around the sides. It can thump.

And it can also jingle.

Tambourine

Tom-tom

Text Marking

Compare a tambourine and a tom-tom.

☐ Draw a box around the signal word **both**.

⬭ Circle one way they are alike.

34

Informational Passages for Text Marking & Close Reading: Grade 1
© 2015 by Scholastic Teaching Resources

Passage 12: Two Ways to Fly

1. A; Sample answer: The article says this in the third sentence.

2. C; Sample answer: I picked C because that is the main way a glider is not like an airplane.

3. Sample answer: Airplanes have engines so they can go faster and farther.

12 Compare & Contrast   Name _____   Date _____

Two Ways to Fly

Read the transportation article.
Then follow the directions in the box.

Both **airplanes** and **gliders**

fly in the sky. Both have wings.

Both have pilots. But they are different

in a very important way.

Airplanes have engines, but gliders do not.

So how do gliders fly?

An airplane pulls a glider into the air.

They go higher and higher together.

Then the airplane lets go. The glider floats alone.

The pilot guides it home. It lands safely.

Text Marking

Contrast airplanes and gliders.

☐ Draw boxes around the signal words **but** and **different**.

___ Underline one way they are different.

An airplane towing a glider with a rope

36

Informational Passages for Text Marking & Close Reading: Grade 1
© 2015 by Scholastic Teaching Resources

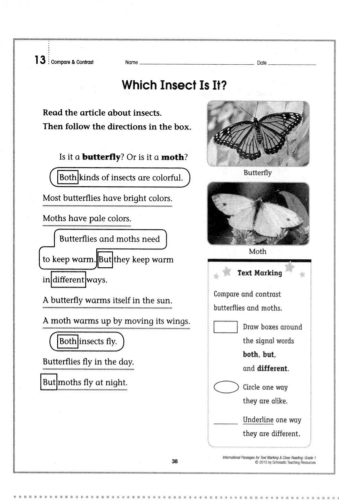

Passage 13: Which Insect Is It?

1. B; Sample answer: The article is about how moths and butterflies are the same and different.

2. B; Sample answers: It says in paragraph 3 that a moth warms up by moving its wings.

3. Answers will vary. Check that students' responses are different from what they underlined in the article.

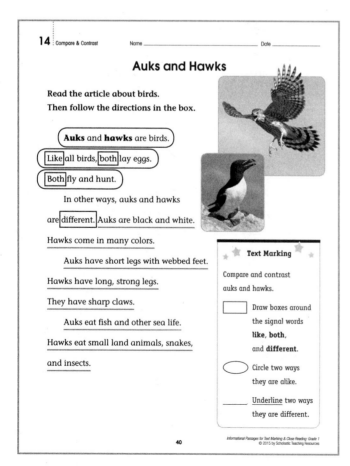

Passage 14: Auks and Hawks

1. C; Sample answer: The article compares and contrasts two kinds of birds—auks and hawks.

2. B; Sample answer: The article says this in the first paragraph.

3. Sample answers: The hawk is on the top. I can see its sharp claws. The auk is at the bottom. I can see its webbed feet.

Informational Passages for Text Marking & Close Reading: Grade 1
© 2015 by Scholastic Teaching Resources

Name _____ Date _____

High Waters

Read the earth science article.
Then follow the directions in the box.

A **flood** happens when water spills over.
What causes a flood?

Snow melts off mountains in the spring.

It turns into water.

The water runs downhill.

It flows into rivers.

Rainstorms add more water to rivers.

Rivers can't hold all that extra water.

So they **overflow**.

The water covers everything nearby.

Floods soak fields, roads, and towns.

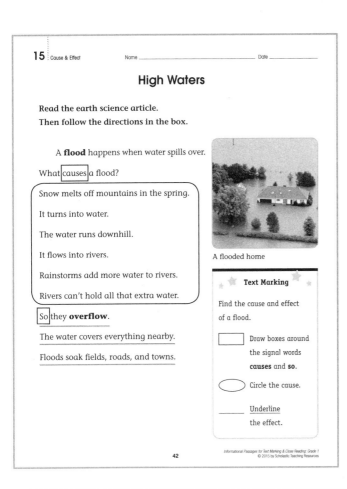

A flooded home

★ **Text Marking** ★

Find the cause and effect
of a flood.

☐ Draw boxes around
the signal words
causes and **so**.

◯ Circle the cause.

___ Underline
the effect.

Informational Passages for Text Marking & Close Reading: Grade 1
© 2015 by Scholastic Teaching Resources

◀ Sample Text Markings

Passage 15: High Waters

1. B; Sample answer: The article says that when rivers can't hold extra water, they overflow. And the first sentence says that a flood happens when water spills over.

2. C; Sample answer: The article says that melting snow and rain can cause floods. Floods happen to fields and towns.

3. Sample answer: In spring, it gets warmer and that would make snow melt and turn into water.

Name _____ Date _____

Ahhh...choo!

Read the health article.
Then follow the directions in the box.

Almost anything can cause a sneeze.

You might breathe in some dust,
cold air, or even pepper.

It tickles the inside of your nose.

So you need to clear it out.

Your brain gets the message.

It signals some muscles to get ready
to help. When they do, you suddenly feel
the results. Your eyes close tight.

Your mouth opens, and you sneeze:

AHHH...CHOO! The tickle is gone.

★ **Text Marking** ★

Find the cause and effects.

☐ Draw boxes around
the signal words
cause and **results**.

◯ Circle the cause.

___ Underline
the effects.

Informational Passages for Text Marking & Close Reading: Grade 1
© 2015 by Scholastic Teaching Resources

◀ Sample Text Markings

Passage 16: Ahhh...choo!

1. A; Sample answer: It says this at the beginning of the second paragraph.

2. C; Sample answer: I picked C because I read the other two choices in the article.

3. Sample answer: Sneezing gets rid of a tickle inside my nose.

Informational Passages for Text Marking & Close Reading: Grade 1
© 2015 by Scholastic Teaching Resources

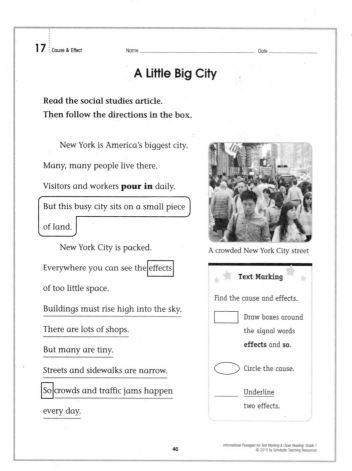

Passage 17: A Little Big City

1. C; Sample answer: This is the main idea of this article.

2. B; Sample answer: I picked B because it makes sense from the article that many people come to the city at one time.

3. Sample answer: New York is big because of how many people live and visit there, not because of how much space it takes up.

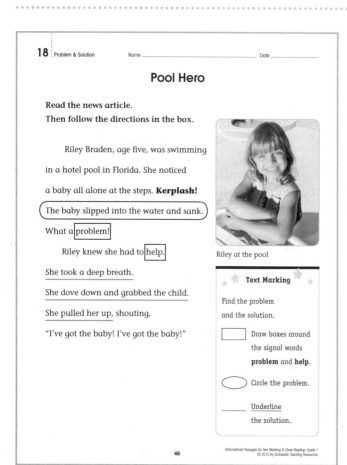

Passage 18: Pool Hero

1. B; Sample answer: That is how it sounded when the baby fell into the pool.

2. C; Sample answer: A young baby probably couldn't swim. Riley knew this was a bad problem and rushed to help.

3. Sample answer: I think Riley tried hard to let the baby's family know she was okay, and to make sure they came to help.

Informational Passages for Text Marking & Close Reading: Grade 1
© 2015 by Scholastic Teaching Resources

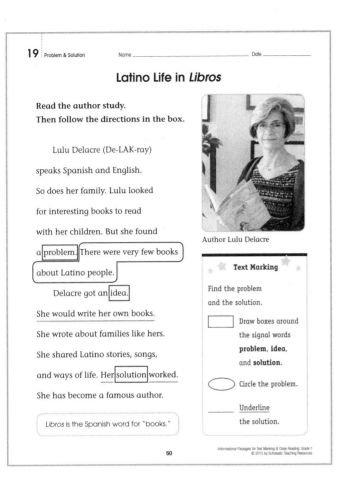

Passage 19: Latino Life in *Libros*

1. C; Sample answer: It says in the first sentence that she speaks English and Spanish.

2. A; Sample answer: The article says that she writes about Latino families like hers.

3. Sample answer: She wrote her own books because she couldn't find good ones about Latino people and their lives. So she solved this problem by becoming an author.

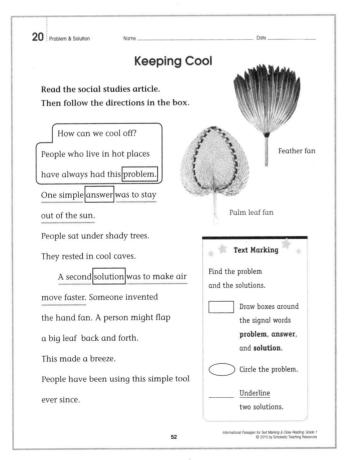

Passage 20: Keeping Cool

1. B; Sample answer: Going in a cave was a way to stay out of the sun and keep cool.

2. A; Sample answer: I picked A because the article said this in the second paragraph.

3. Sample answer: Both have handles. Both look flat. And both are made from things in nature—plants and feathers.

Notes

Informational Passages for Text Marking & Close Reading: Grade 1
© 2015 by Scholastic Teaching Resources